Table of Contents

Consonants Review

Say the name of each picture. These words begin with letter sound b.

Print the letter b at the beginning of each word.

all

at

oat

us

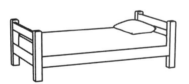ed

ook

Colour the ball	blue	Colour the bus.	yellow
Colour the bat.	black	Colour the bed.	red
Colour the boat.	brown	Colour the book.	green

Say the name of each picture. These words begin with letter sound c.

Print the letter c at the beginning of each word.

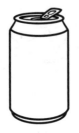

c at   c an   c ap

c ake   c up   c ar

Colour the cat.	yellow	Colour the cake.	purple
Colour the can.	blue	Colour the cup.	brown
Colour the cap.	green	Colour the car.	red

Say the name of each picture. These words begin with letter sound d.

Print the letter d at the beginning of each word.

dog   dress   desk

door   duck   doll

Colour the dog.	black	Colour the door.	brown
Colour the dress.	yellow	Colour the duck.	orange
Colour the desk.	blue	Colour the doll.	green

Say the name of each picture. These words begin with letter sound f. Print the letter f at the beginning of each word.

 an
 ence
 ish

 ork
 oot
frog

Colour the fan. black
Colour the fence. yellow
Colour the fish. blue

Colour the fork. brown
Colour the foot. orange
Colour the frog. green

Say the name of each picture. These words begin with letter sound g.

Print the letter g at the beginning of each word.

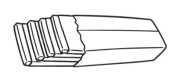

Colour the girl. | green | Colour the gift. | red |
Colour the goat. | blue | Colour the gum. | orange |
Colour the goose. | yellow | Colour the guitar. | brown |

Consonant Review: H

Say the name of each picture. These words begin with letter sound h.
Print the letter h at the beginning of each word.

hat   hand   house

hen   heart   hippo

Colour the hat. — black	Colour the hen. — brown
Colour the hand. — yellow	Colour the heart. — red
Colour the house. — blue	Colour the hippo. — green

Say the name of each picture. These words begin with letter sound j.
Print the letter j at the beginning of each word.

 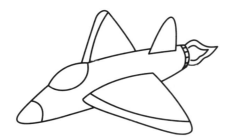 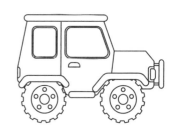

ar   et   eep

ug   elly   am

Colour the jar.	blue	Colour the jug.	brown
Colour the jet.	red	Colour the jelly.	orange
Colour the jeep.	green	Colour the jam.	purple

Consonant Review: K

Say the name of each picture. These words begin with letter sound k.
Print the letter k at the beginning of each word.

kite

kitten

key

king

kettle

kiwi

Colour the kite. ⟨▌black ▌⟩	Colour the king. ⟨▌brown ▌⟩
Colour the kitten. ⟨▌yellow ▌⟩	Colour the kettle. ⟨▌orange ▌⟩
Colour the key. ⟨▌blue ▌⟩	Colour the kiwi. ⟨▌green ▌⟩

Say the name of each picture. These words begin with letter sound l.

Print the letter l at the beginning of each word.

ion

ock

amb

og

eaf

amp

Colour the lion.	red	Colour the log.	brown
Colour the lock.	black	Colour the leaf.	green
Colour the lamb.	purple	Colour the lamp.	blue

Consonant Review: M

Say the name of each picture. These words begin with letter sound m.
Print the letter m at the beginning of each word.

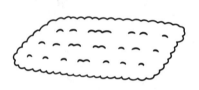

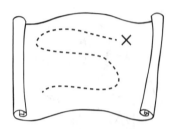

mat moon map

mop milk mouse

Colour the mat.	yellow	Colour the mop.	brown
Colour the moon.	blue	Colour the milk.	orange
Colour the map.	red	Colour the mouse.	green

Say the name of each picture. These words begin with letter sound n.

Print the letter n at the beginning of each word.

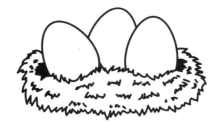

net

nest

nut

nail

nose

note

Colour the net.	black	Colour the nail.	blue
Colour the nest.	yellow	Colour the nose.	red
Colour the nut.	brown	Colour the note.	green

Say the name of each picture. These words begin with letter sound p.

Print the letter p at the beginning of each word.

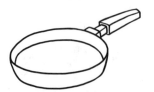

Colour the paw.	black	Colour the pail.	purple
Colour the pan.	blue	Colour the pig.	orange
Colour the pie.	red	Colour the pen.	green

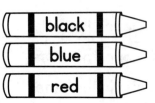

Consonant Review: Q

Say the name of each picture. These words begin with letter sound q.
Print the letter q at the beginning of each word.

queen   quail   quilt

quill   question

Colour the queen. [yellow]   Colour the quill. [brown]
Colour the quail. [red]   Colour the
Colour the quilt. [blue]   question mark. [orange]

Consonant Review: R

Say the name of each picture. These words begin with letter sound r.
Print the letter r at the beginning of each word.

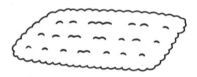

rat   rain   rug

rake   ring   rose

Colour the rat. (black)   Colour the rake. (brown)
Colour the rain. (yellow)   Colour the ring. (orange)
Colour the rug. (blue)   Colour the rose. (green)

Say the name of each picture. These words begin with letter sound s.

Print the letter s at the beginning of each word.

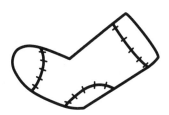

Colour the sun.	orange	Colour the sock.	brown
Colour the saw.	blue	Colour the snake.	red
Colour the spoon.	green	Colour the soap.	yellow

Consonant Review: T

Say the name of each picture. These words begin with letter sound t.

Print tho lottor t at tho boginning of' oaoh word.

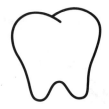

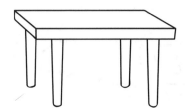

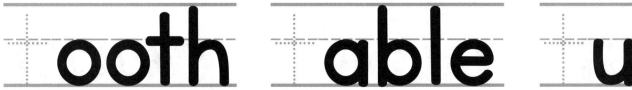

ooth   able   ub

   op   rain    ree

Colour the tooth. (blue)   Colour the top. (orange)
Colour the table. (yellow)   Colour the train. (purple)
Colour the tub. (red)   Colour the tree. (green)

Say the name of each picture. These words begin with letter sound v.

Print the letter v at the beginning of each word.

vase   vest   violin

vulture   van   vine

Colour the vase.	red	Colour the vulture.	brown
Colour the vest.	yellow	Colour the van.	black
Colour the violin.	blue	Colour the vine.	green

Consonant Review: W

Say the name of each picture. These words begin with letter sound w.
Print the letter w at the beginning of each word.

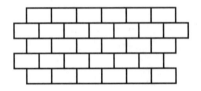

web walrus wall

well worm wagon

Colour the web.	black	Colour the well.	green
Colour the walrus.	blue	Colour the worm.	yellow
Colour the wall.	red	Colour the wagon.	purple

Say the name of each picture. These words begin with letter sound x.

Print the letter x at the beginning of each word.

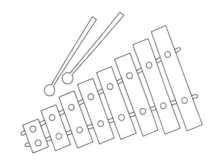

x-ray

xylophone

x-ray fish

Colour the x-ray. ⬜ black ⬜   Colour the x-ray fish. ⬜ yellow ⬜

Colour the xylophone. ⬜ blue ⬜

Say the name of each picture. These words begin with letter sound y. Print the letter y at the beginning of each word.

y arn

y am

y o-yo

y olk

y ak

y eti

Colour the yarn. **orange**	Colour the yolk. **yellow**
Colour the yam. **red**	Colour the yak. **brown**
Colour the yo-yo. **blue**	Colour the yeti. **green**

Say the name of each picture. These words begin with letter sound z.

Print the letter z at the beginning of each word.

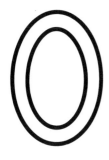  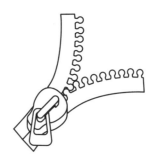

ero oo ipper

ebra ucchini

Colour the zero. ⟨ black ⟩ Colour the zebra. ⟨ brown ⟩

Colour the zoo. ⟨ yellow ⟩ Colour the zucchini. ⟨ green ⟩

Colour the zipper. ⟨ blue ⟩

Short and Long Vowels

Long vowels say their own name. Short vowels make different sounds. Read the examples below, say the name of the pictures out loud.

a

short ă

jam

long ā

cave

e

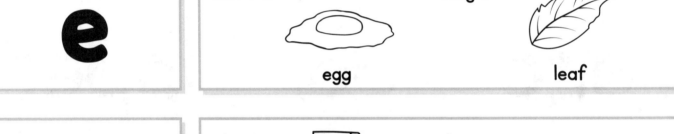

short ĕ

egg

long ē

leaf

i

short ĭ

milk

long ī

pie

o

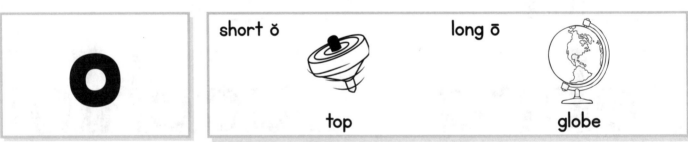

short ŏ

top

long ō

globe

u

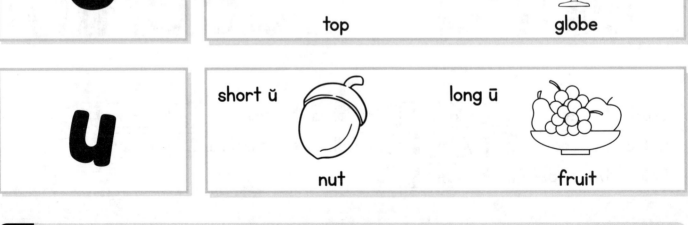

short ŭ

nut

long ū

fruit

Short Vowels

Say the name of each picture out loud. Listen for the short ā sound. Use the colour key to colour the pictures.

fan

cat

map

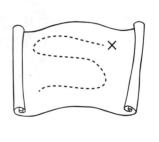

cap

jam

bag

Colour the fan. | purple |
Colour the cat. | brown |
Colour the map. | yellow |

Colour the cap. | blue |
Colour the jam. | red |
Colour the bag. | green |

Short Vowel Practice: a

Say the name of each picture out loud. Listen for the short ā sound. Use the colour key to colour the pictures.

pan

cab

rat

bat

hat

can

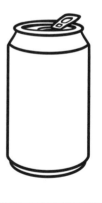

Colour the pan.	black	Colour the bat.	brown
Colour the cab.	yellow	Colour the hat.	orange
Colour the rat.	blue	Colour the can.	green

Short Vowel Practice: a

Say the name of the pictures out loud. Fill in the missing vowel for each of the words. Use the colour key to colour the pictures.

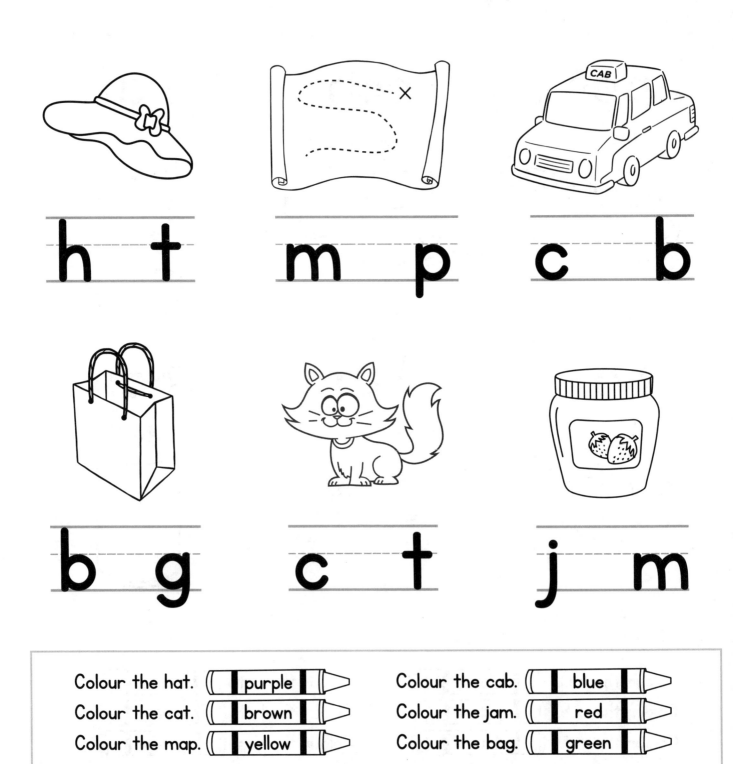

h __ t   m __ p   c __ b

b __ g   c __ t   j __ m

Colour the hat. purple	Colour the cab. blue
Colour the cat. brown	Colour the jam. red
Colour the map. yellow	Colour the bag. green

Short Vowel Practice: a

Say the name of the pictures out loud. Fill in the missing vowel for each of the words. Use the colour key to colour the pictures.

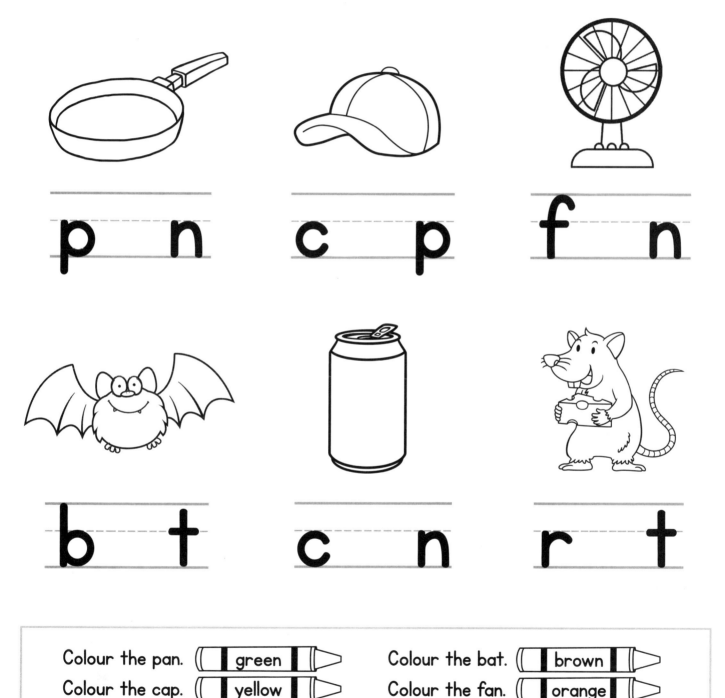

p ___ n   c ___ p   f ___ n

b ___ t   c ___ n   r ___ t

Colour the pan.	green	Colour the bat.	brown
Colour the cap.	yellow	Colour the fan.	orange
Colour the rat.	blue	Colour the can.	black

Say the name of the pictures out loud.
Draw a line from each picture to the matching word.

jam

hat

bag

bat

map

cat

Say the name of the pictures out loud.
Draw a line from each picture to the matching word.

can

rat

cab

pan

cap

fan

Short Vowel Practice: a

Say the name of the pictures out loud.
Find the words. Look across for the words. Circle the words.

bat   cat   rat   hat   jam   bag

b	a	g	c	l	w	e
v	d	k	c	a	t	r
r	a	t	f	o	q	d
s	c	n	e	j	a	m
h	a	t	r	w	b	p
k	c	n	b	a	t	q

Short Vowel Practice: a

Say the name of the pictures out loud.
Find the words. Look across for the words. Circle the words.

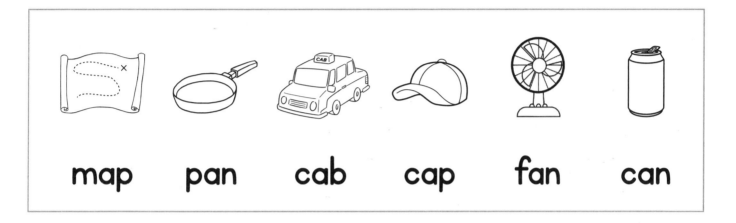

map   pan   cab   cap   fan   can

z c a n l s d

u o f p a n j

c a b l e w g

k r p b f a n

e c a p w s z

m a p i v p s

Short Vowel Practice: e

Say the name of each picture out loud. Listen for the short ĕ sound. Use the colour key to colour the pictures.

gem

leg

hen

bed

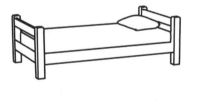

egg

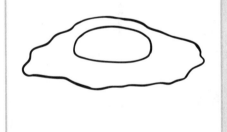

jet

Colour the gem. — blue   Colour the bed. — orange

Colour the leg. — red   Colour the egg. — green

Colour the hen. — yellow   Colour the jet. — black

Short Vowel Practice: e

Say the name of each picture out loud. Listen for the short ĕ sound. Use the colour key to colour the pictures.

well

nest
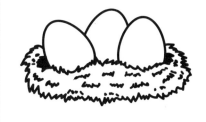

pen

ten

vest

net

Colour the well. (black)   Colour the ten. (green)

Colour the nest. (brown)   Colour the vest. (red)

Colour the pen. (purple)   Colour the net. (orange)

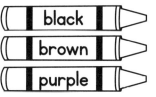

Short Vowel Practice: e

Say the name of the pictures out loud. Fill in the missing vowel for each of the words. Use the colour key to colour the pictures

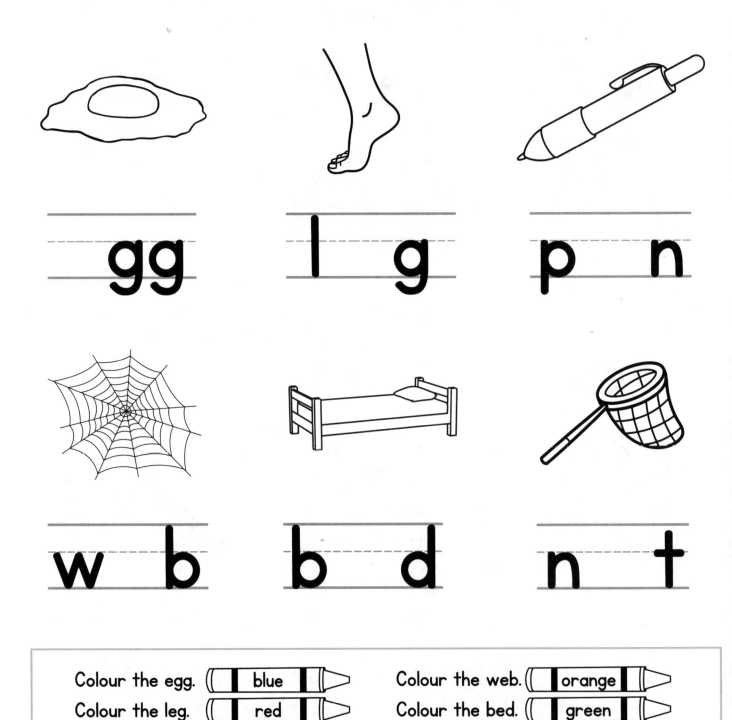

g g   l   g   p   n

w   b   b   d   n   t

Colour the egg.	blue	Colour the web.	orange
Colour the leg.	red	Colour the bed.	green
Colour the pen.	yellow	Colour the net.	black

Short Vowel Practice: e

Say the name of the pictures out loud. Fill in the missing vowel for each of the words. Use the colour key to colour the pictures.

j_t   t_n   v_st

w_ll   h_n   g_m

Colour the jet. | black   Colour the well. | green
Colour the ten. | brown   Colour the hen. | red
Colour the vest. | purple   Colour the gem. | orange

Short Vowel Practice: e

Say the name of the pictures out loud.
Draw a line from each picture to the matching word.

   leg

   bed

   pen

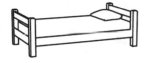   egg

   net

   web

Short Vowel Practice: e

Say the name of the pictures out loud.
Draw a line from each picture to the matching word.

jet

vest

well

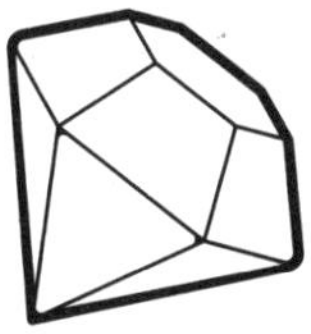

ten

gem

hen

Short Vowel Practice: e

Say the name of the pictures out loud.
Find the words. Look across for the words. Circle the words.

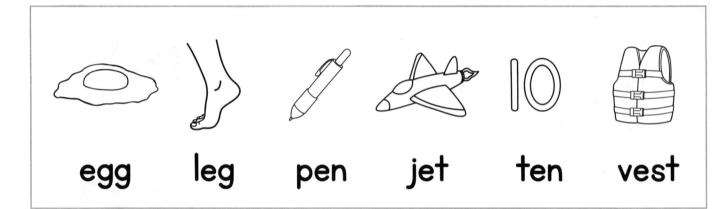

egg   leg   pen   jet   ten   vest

b	a	e	g	g	w	e
v	d	p	e	n	t	r
r	j	e	t	o	q	d
s	c	n	l	e	g	t
f	t	e	n	w	b	p
k	c	n	v	e	s	t

Short Vowel Practice: e

Say the name of the pictures out loud.
Find the words. Look across for the words. Circle the words.

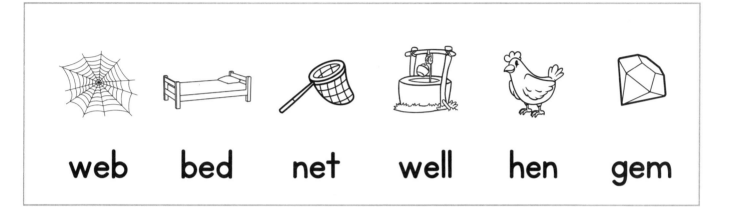

web   bed   net   well   hen   gem

z   m   w   e   b   s   d

u   p   b   e   d   f   k

w   e   l   l   g   h   p

k   r   p   h   e   n   p

e   f   n   e   t   s   z

c   g   e   m   v   p   s

Short Vowel Practice: i

Say the name of each picture out loud. Listen for the short i sound. Use the colour key to colour the pictures.

six

6

mitten

king

milk

igloo

pin

Colour the six. (red)
Colour the mitten. (brown)
Colour the king. (yellow)

Colour the milk. (blue)
Colour the igloo. (purple)
Colour the pin. (green)

Short Vowel Practice: i

Say the name of each picture out loud. Listen for the short ĭ sound. Use the colour key to colour the pictures.

kid

kitten

fish

fin

gift

pig

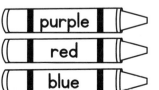

Colour the kid. | purple

Colour the kitten. | red

Colour the fish. | blue

Colour the fin. | green

Colour the gift. | orange

Colour the pig. | pink

Say the name of the pictures out loud. Fill in the missing vowel for each of the words. Use the colour key to colour the pictures.

s x

m tten

k ng

m lk

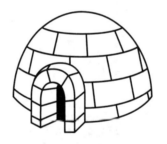

gloo

p n

Colour the six.	red	Colour the milk.	blue
Colour the mitten.	brown	Colour the igloo.	purple
Colour the king.	yellow	Colour the pin.	green

Short Vowel Practice: i

Say the name of the pictures out loud. Fill in the missing vowel for each of the words. Use the colour key to colour the pictures.

k d   k tten   f sh

f n   g ft   p g

Colour the kid.	purple	Colour the fin.	green
Colour the kitten.	red	Colour the gift.	orange
Colour the fish.	blue	Colour the pig.	yellow

Short Vowel Practice: i

Say the name of the pictures out loud.
Draw a line from each picture to the matching word.

kid

milk

mitten

king

fish

six

Short Vowel Practice: i

Say the name of the pictures out loud.
Draw a line from each picture to the matching word.

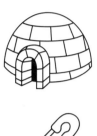

fin

gift

kitten

pig

igloo

pin

Short Vowel Practice: i

Say the name of the pictures out loud.
Find the words. Look across for the words. Circle the words.

six   mitten   king   fin   igloo   pin

u k l p i n e

i g l o o n r

a p k i n g d

s f i n q w h

m i t t e n p

k c n b s i x

Short Vowel Practice: i

Say the name of the pictures out loud.
Find the words. Look across for the words. Circle the words.

kid   milk   fish   gift   kitten   pig

k	i	d	l	a	v	d
u	j	i	p	i	g	j
g	i	f	t	e	w	g
j	r	f	i	s	h	c
z	k	i	t	t	e	n
t	m	i	l	k	l	s

Short Vowel Practice: o

Say the name of each picture out loud. Listen for the short ŏ sound. Use the colour key to colour the pictures.

log

top

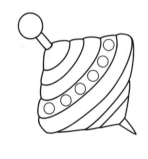

hog

doll

mop

box

Colour the log. 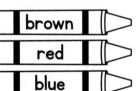 brown   Colour the doll. yellow

Colour the top. red   Colour the mop. purple

Colour the hog. blue   Colour the box. green

Short Vowel Practice: o

sock

fox

frog

pot

dog

rod
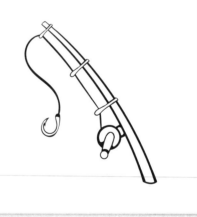

Colour the sock.　black　　Colour the pot.　red

Colour the fox.　orange　　Colour the dog.　brown

Colour the frog.　green　　Colour the rod.　yellow

Short Vowel Practice: o

Say the name of the pictures out loud. Fill in the missing vowel for each of the words. Use the colour key to colour the pictures.

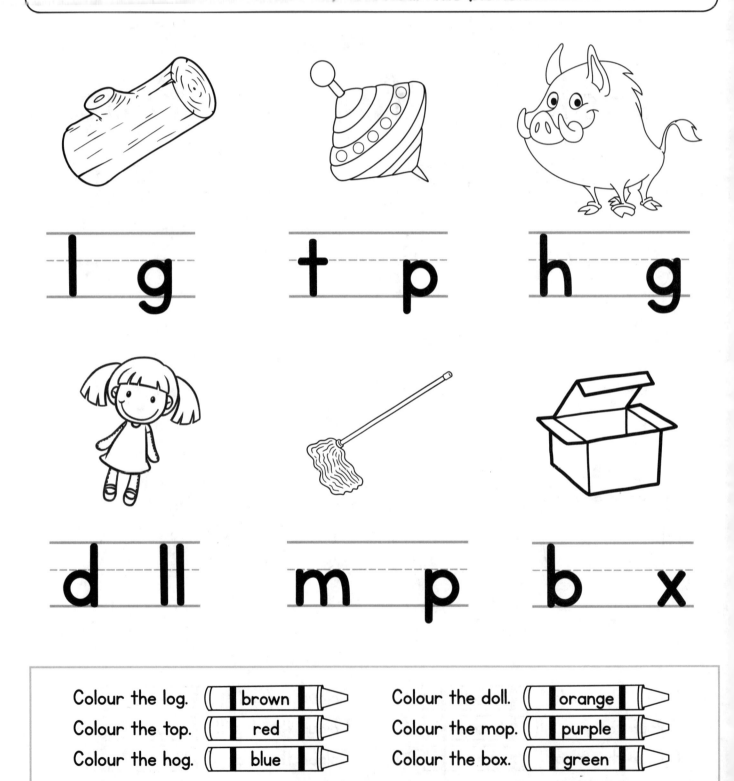

l __ g

t __ p

h __ g

d __ ll

m __ p

b __ x

Colour the log. | brown
Colour the top. | red
Colour the hog. | blue

Colour the doll. | orange
Colour the mop. | purple
Colour the box. | green

Say the name of the pictures out loud. Fill in the missing vowel for each of the words. Use the colour key to colour the pictures.

s __ ck

f __ x

fr __ g

p __ t

d __ g

r __ d

Colour the sock. | black
Colour the fox. | orange
Colour the frog. | green

Colour the pot. | red
Colour the dog. | brown
Colour the rod. | yellow

Short Vowel Practice: o

Say the name of the pictures out loud.
Draw a line from each picture to the matching word.

fox

hog

frog

top

log

sock

Say the name of the pictures out loud.
Draw a line from each picture to the matching word.

pot

rod

dog

doll

mop

box

Say the name of the pictures out loud.
Find the words. Look across for the words. Circle the words.

log   top   hog   sock   fox   frog

b t o p f o x

v d l o g a r

r f r o g q d

d b s o c k t

z y x e w b p

k f h o g a x

Short Vowel Practice: o

Say the name of the pictures out loud.
Find the words. Look across for the words. Circle the words.

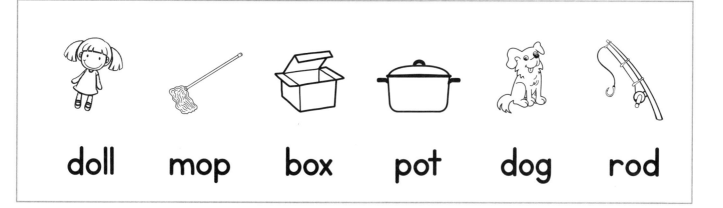

doll　　mop　　box　　pot　　dog　　rod

z　m　d　o　l　l　w

r　o　d　k　d　f　k

q　u　x　s　b　o　g

k　r　p　o　t　a　s

e　b　o　x　h　y　u

c　e　m　o　p　r　k

Say the name of each picture out loud. Listen for the short u sound. Use the colour key to colour the pictures.

pup

drum

bus

tub

jug

bug

Colour the pup. 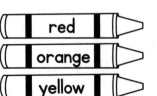 red

Colour the drum. orange

Colour the bus. yellow

Colour the tub. 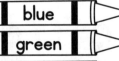 blue

Colour the jug. green

Colour the bug. purple

Short Vowel Practice: u

Say the name of each picture out loud. Listen for the short ŭ sound. Use the colour key to colour the pictures.

sun

cup

nut

hut

plum

duck

Colour the sun. 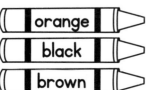 orange
Colour the cup. black
Colour the nut. brown

Colour the hut. 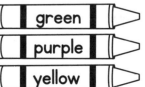 green
Colour the plum. purple
Colour the duck. yellow

Short Vowel Practice: u

Say the name of the pictures out loud. Fill in the missing vowel for each of the words. Use the colour key to colour the pictures.

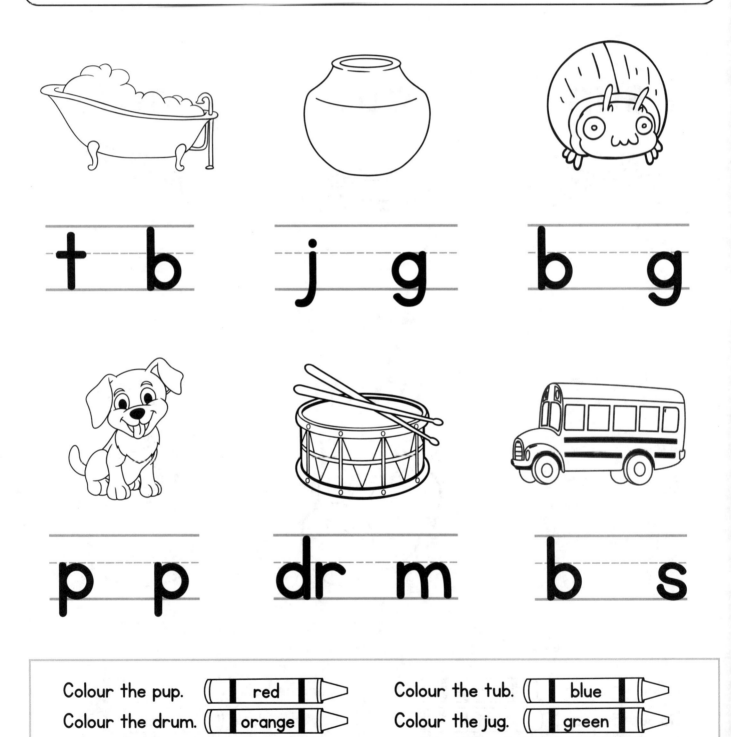

t __ b   j __ g   b __ g

__ p __ p   dr __ m   b __ s

Colour the pup. | red   Colour the tub. | blue

Colour the drum. | orange   Colour the jug. | green

Colour the bus. | yellow   Colour the bug. | purple

Say the name of the pictures out loud. Fill in the missing vowel for each of the words. Use the colour key to colour the pictures.

h __ t   pl __ m   d __ ck

s __ n   c __ p   n __ t

Colour the sun.	orange	Colour the hut.	green
Colour the cup.	black	Colour the plum.	purple
Colour the nut.	brown	Colour the duck.	yellow

Short Vowel Practice: u

Say the name of the pictures out loud.
Draw a line from each picture to the matching word.

jug

duck

plum

bug

hut

tub

Say the name of the pictures out loud.
Draw a line from each picture to the matching word.

 bus

 sun

 drum

 cup

 pup

 nut

Short Vowel Practice: u

Say the name of the pictures out loud.
Find the words. Look across for the words. Circle the words.

| tub | jug | bug | hut | plum | duck |

t	u	b	p	l	u	m
v	j	u	g	a	t	r
r	h	e	d	u	c	k
s	c	n	e	b	u	g
p	j	u	g	q	b	p
w	h	u	t	w	c	n

Short Vowel Practice: u

Say the name of the pictures out loud.
Find the words. Look across for the words. Circle the words.

pup   drum   bus   sun   cup   nut

z	p	c	u	p	s	d
u	p	d	r	u	m	j
b	u	s	l	r	w	g
k	r	p	b	n	u	t
e	f	p	u	p	s	z
c	s	u	n	v	h	b

Rhyming Words

Say the name of each picture out loud. Print the beginning sound to complete the word. Circle the letters that make the pair of words rhyme.

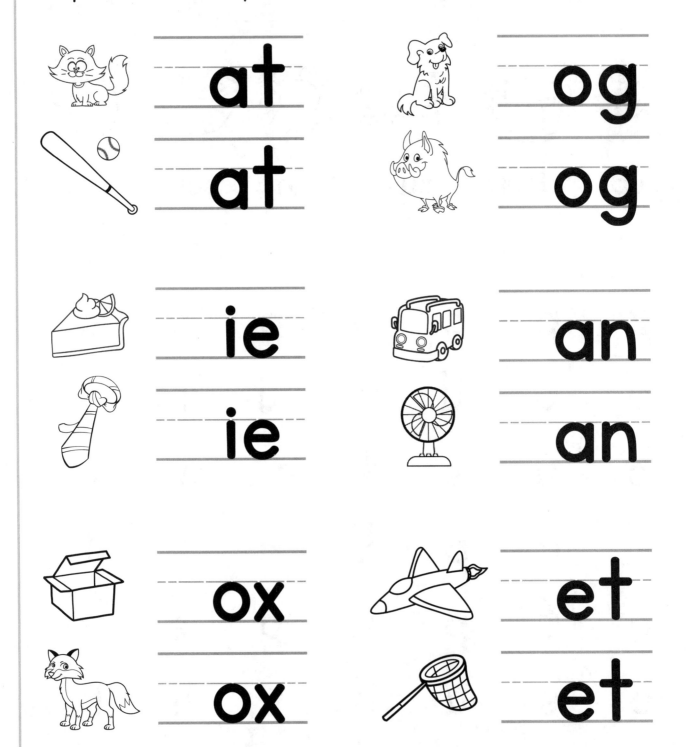

at

at

og

og

ie

ie

an

an

ox

ox

et

et

Long Vowels

ā ē ī ō ū

Long Vowel Practice: a

Say the name of each picture out loud. Listen for the long ā sound. Use the colour key to colour the pictures.

tape	vase	ape
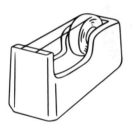		
cane	**wave**	**cave**

Colour the tape. 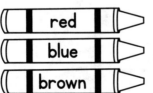 red   Colour the cane. 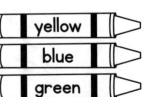 yellow

Colour the vase. blue   Colour the wave. blue

Colour the ape. brown   Colour the cave. green

Long Vowel Practice: a

Say the name of each picture out loud. Listen for the long ā sound. Use the colour key to colour the pictures.

cage

game
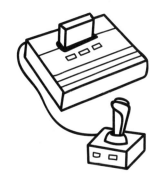

rake

mane

plate

cake

Colour the cage. 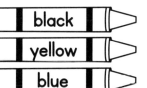 black
Colour the game. yellow
Colour the rake. blue

Colour the mane. 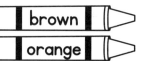 brown
Colour the plate. orange
Colour the cake. purple

Long Vowel Practice: a

Say the name of each picture out loud. Fill in the missing vowel.
Use the colour key to colour the pictures.

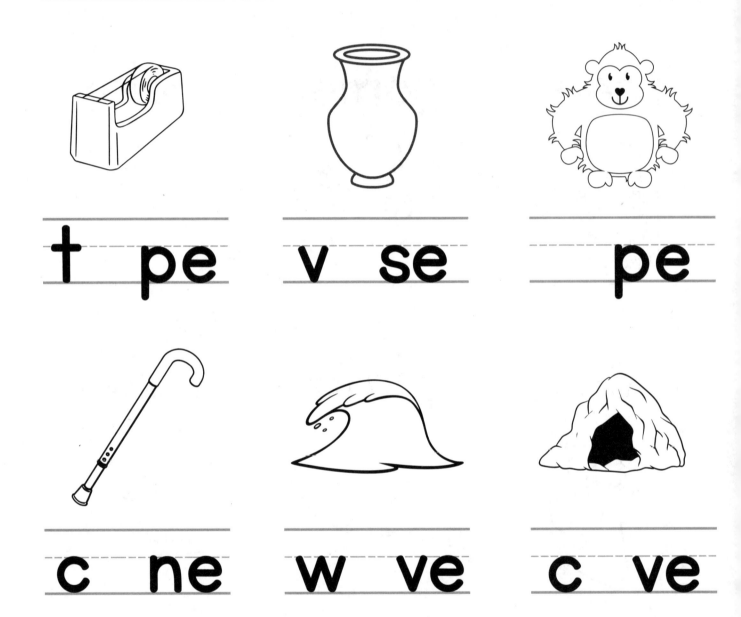

t __ pe   v __ se   __ pe

c __ ne   w __ ve   c __ ve

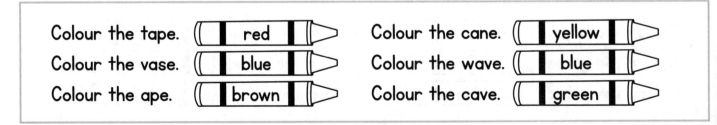

Colour the tape.	red	Colour the cane.	yellow
Colour the vase.	blue	Colour the wave.	blue
Colour the ape.	brown	Colour the cave.	green

Say the name of each picture out loud. Fill in the missing vowel.
Use the colour key to colour the pictures.

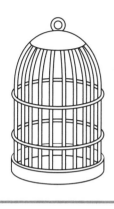
c ___ ge

g ___ me

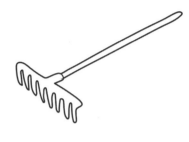
r ___ ke

m ___ ne

pl ___ te

c ___ ke

Colour the cage.	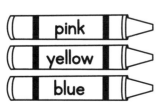 pink	Colour the mane.	brown
Colour the game.	yellow	Colour the plate.	orange
Colour the rake.	blue	Colour the cake.	purple

Say the name of each picture out loud.
Draw a line from each picture to the matching word.

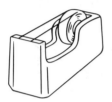

game

tape

rake

vase

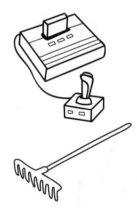

cage

ape

Say the name of each picture out loud.
Draw a line from each picture to the matching word.

wave

plate

mane

cake

cave

cane

Read the words in the word box out loud. Read each sentence.
Fill in the blank with a word from the word box.

| vase | tape | plate | ape | cave |

I put _____ on the box.

I saw an _____ at the zoo.

The _____ is pretty.

The _____ is clean.

The _____ is dark.

Read each word out loud. Print the word.
Circle the picture that matches the word.

tape
_____
_____

vase
_____
_____

ape
_____
_____

cage
_____
_____

game
_____
_____

rake
_____
_____

Long Vowel Practice: e

Say the name of each picture out loud. Listen for the long ē sound. Use the colour key to colour the pictures.

bee

tree

seal

jeep
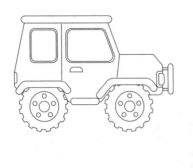

feet
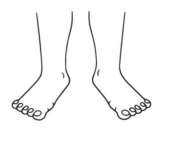

seed

Colour the bee.	yellow	Colour the jeep.	red
Colour the tree.	green	Colour the feet.	orange
Colour the seal.	blue	Colour the seed.	brown

Long Vowel Practice: e

Say the name of each picture out loud. Listen for the long ē sound. Use the colour key to colour the pictures.

sheep

deer

ear

meal

leaf

beak

Colour the sheep.	black	Colour the meal.	red
Colour the deer.	green	Colour the leaf.	brown
Colour the ear.	blue	Colour the beak.	yellow

Long Vowel Practice: e

Say the name of each picture out loud. Fill in the missing vowel for each of the words. Use the colour key to colour the pictures.

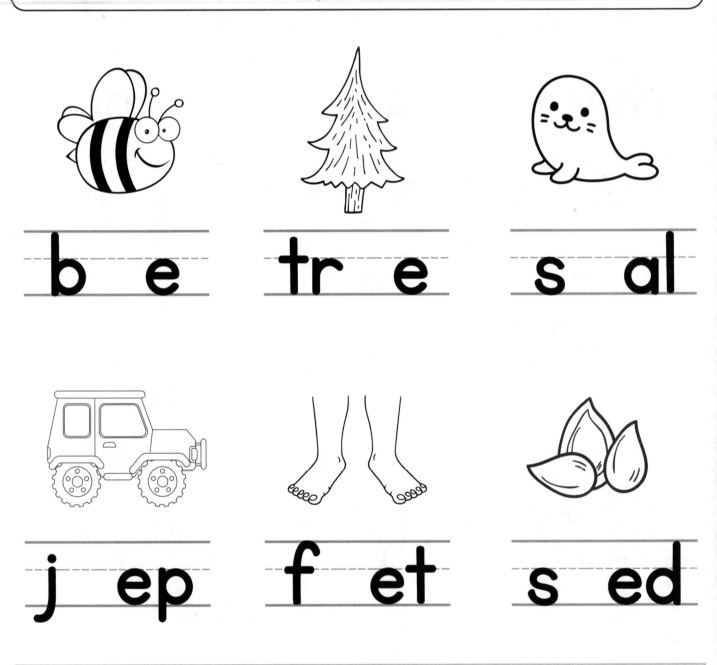

b e   tr e   s al

j ep   f et   s ed

Colour the bee.   yellow   Colour the jeep.   red
Colour the tree.   green   Colour the feet.   orange
Colour the seal.   blue   Colour the seed.   brown

Long Vowel Practice: e

Say the name of each picture out loud. Fill in the missing vowel for each of the words. Use the colour key to colour the pictures.

sh ep

d er

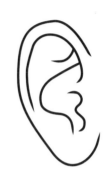

ar

m al

l af

b ak

Colour the sheep.	black	Colour the meal.	red
Colour the deer.	green	Colour the leaf.	brown
Colour the ear.	blue	Colour the beak.	yellow

Long Vowel Practice: e

Say the name of each picture out loud.
Draw a line from each picture to the matching word.

tree

sheep

deer

ear

bee

seal

Long Vowel Practice: e

Say the name of each picture out loud.
Draw a line from each picture to the matching word.

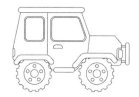

feet

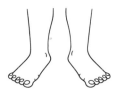

jeep

meal

leaf

beak

seed

Long Vowel Practice: e

seed	seal	bee	tree	jeep

The _____ makes honey.

I saw a _____ at the zoo.

I have two _____ .

The _____ is fast.

The _____ is tall.

Long Vowel Practice: e

Read each word out loud. Print the word.
Circle the picture that matches the word.

sheep

bee

jeep

seed

deer

beak

Long Vowel Practice: i

Say the name of each picture out loud. Circle long vowel ī.
Use the colour key to colour the pictures.

ice	dice	tire
	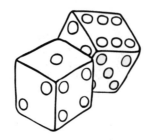	

nine	fire	five

Colour the ice. blue
Colour the dice. red
Colour the tire. black

Colour the nine. green
Colour the fire. orange
Colour the five. purple

Say the name of each picture out loud. Circle long vowel ī.
Use the colour key to colour the pictures.

slide

vine

bride

pie

dime

hive

Colour the slide. 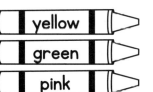 yellow   Colour the pie.  brown

Colour the vine. green   Colour the dime. red

Colour the bride. pink   Colour the hive. orange

Long Vowel Practice: i

Say the name of each picture out loud. Fill in the missing vowel for each of the words. Use the colour key to colour the pictures.

___ce   d___ce   t___re

n___ne   f___re   f___ve

Colour the ice.	blue	Colour the nine.	green
Colour the dice.	red	Colour the fire.	orange
Colour the tire.	black	Colour the five.	purple

Long Vowel Practice: i

Say the name of each picture out loud. Fill in the missing vowel for each of the words. Use the colour key to colour the pictures.

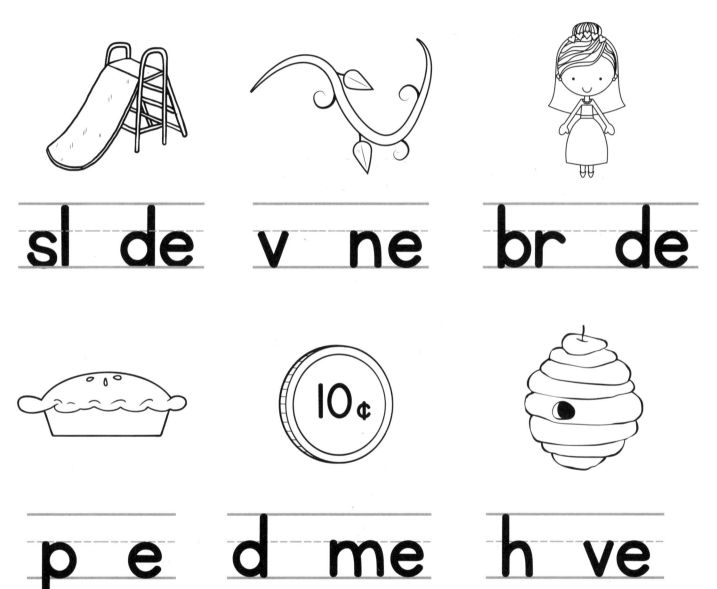

sl__de   v__ne   br__de

p__e   d__me   h__ve

Colour the slide. | yellow | Colour the pie. | brown |

Colour the vine. | green | Colour the dime. | red |

Colour the bride. | purple | Colour the hive. | orange |

Long Vowel Practice: i

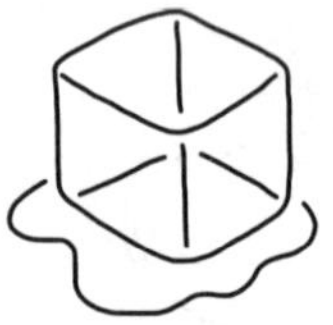

dice

tire

vine

bride

slide

ice

Say the name of each picture out loud.
Draw a line from each picture to the matching word.

dime

hive

nine

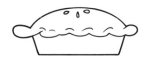

fire

five

pie

Long Vowel Practice: i

pie   slide   dime   fire   ice

I have a _____ .

I like _____ .

The _____ is fun.

The _____ is cold.

The _____ is hot.

Long Vowel Practice: i

Read each word out loud. Print the word.
Circle the picture that matches the word.

slide
_____

dice
_____

dime
_____

nine
_____

pie
_____

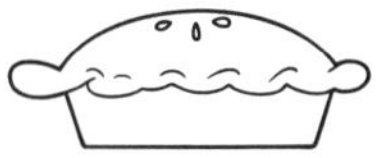

tire
_____

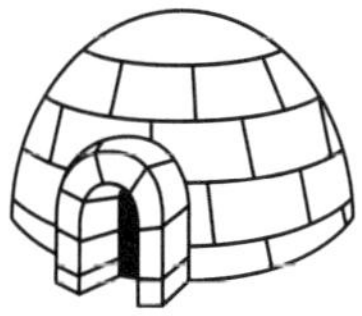

Long Vowel Practice: o

Say the name of each picture out loud. Listen for the long ō sound. Use the colour key to colour the pictures.

robe

rope

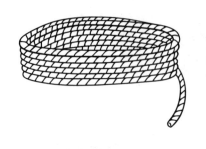

phone

cone

pole

rose

Colour the robe. (blue)   Colour the cone. (green)

Colour the rope. (yellow)   Colour the pole. (purple)

Colour the phone. (black)   Colour the rose. (red)

Long Vowel Practice: o

Say the name of each picture out loud. Listen for the long ō sound. Use the colour key to colour the pictures.

note 	**globe** 	**nose** 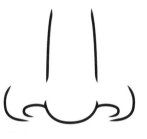
hose 	**bone** 	**stove** 

Colour the note. black
Colour the globe. blue
Colour the nose. red

Colour the hose. brown
Colour the bone. orange
Colour the stove. purple

Long Vowel Practice: o

Say the name of each picture out loud. Fill in the missing vowel for each of the words. Use the colour key to colour the pictures.

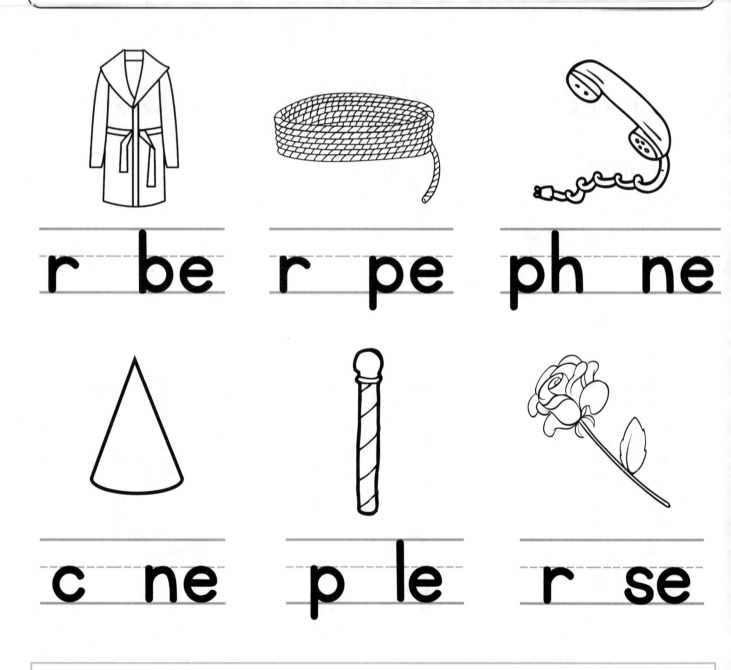

r __ be   r __ pe   ph __ ne

c __ ne   p __ le   r __ se

Colour the robe.	green	Colour the cone.	blue
Colour the rope.	yellow	Colour the pole.	purple
Colour the phone.	orange	Colour the rose.	red

Say the name of each picture out loud. Fill in the missing vowel for each of the words. Use the colour key to colour the pictures.

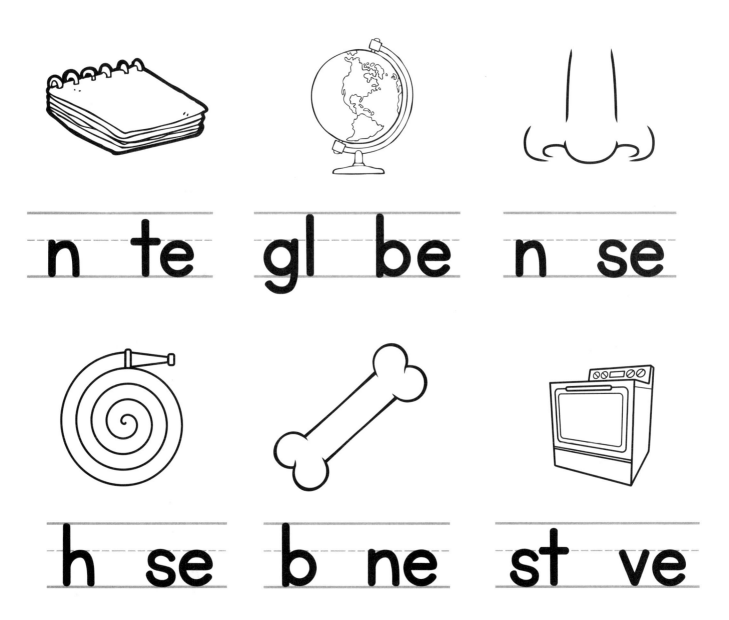

n __ te   gl __ be   n __ se

h __ se   b __ ne   st __ ve

Colour the note. || black || Colour the hose. || brown ||
Colour the globe. || blue || Colour the bone. || orange ||
Colour the nose. || red || Colour the stove. || purple ||

Say the name of each picture out loud.
Draw a line from each picture to the matching word.

phone

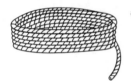

robe

rope

globe

nose

cone

Say the name of each picture out loud.
Draw a line from each picture to the matching word.

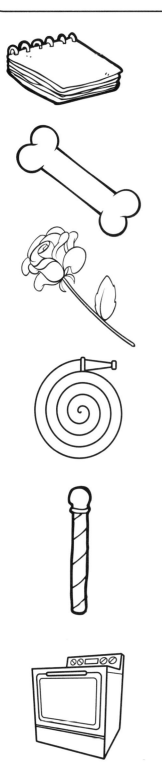

stove

hose

bone

note

rose

pole

Long Vowel Practice: o

Read the words in the word box out loud. Read each sentence. Fill in the blank with a word from the word box.

| rose | nose | robe | phone | rope |

I smell with my _____ .

My _____ is cozy.

I talk on the _____ .

The _____ is pretty.

The _____ is long.

Long Vowel Practice: o

Read each word out loud. Print the word.
Circle the picture that matches the word.

hose

rose

stove

rope

phone

nose

Long Vowel Practice: u

Say the name of each picture out loud. Listen for the long ū sound. Use the colour key to colour the pictures.

cube
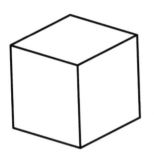

tune

June

mule

ruler
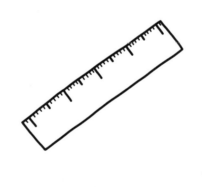

flute

Colour the cube. [purple]
Colour the music. [black]
Colour June. [yellow]

Colour the mule. [brown]
Colour the ruler. [yellow]
Colour the flute. [green]

Long Vowel Practice: u

Say the name of each picture out loud. Listen for the long ū sound. Use the colour key to colour the pictures.

Colour the tube. red
Colour the glue. yellow
Colour the unicycle. orange

Colour the fruit. blue
Colour the unicorn. green
Colour the lute. brown

Long Vowel Practice: u

Say the name of each picture out loud. Fill in the missing vowel for each of the words. Use the colour key to colour the pictures.

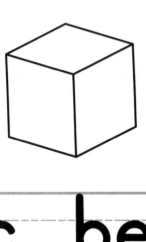

c __ be

t __ ne

J __ ne

m __ le

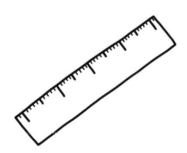

r __ ler

fl __ te

Colour the cube.	purple	
Colour the music.	black	
Colour June.	orange	
Colour the mule.	brown	
Colour the ruler.	yellow	
Colour the flute.	green	

Say the name of each picture out loud. Fill in the missing vowel for each of the words. Use the colour key to colour the pictures.

t be   gl e   nicycle

fr it   nicorn   l te

Colour the tube.	red	
Colour the glue.	yellow	
Colour the unicycle.	orange	

Colour the fruit.	blue	
Colour the unicorn.	green	
Colour the lute.	brown	

Long Vowel Practice: u

Say the name of each picture out loud
Draw a line from each picture to the matching word.

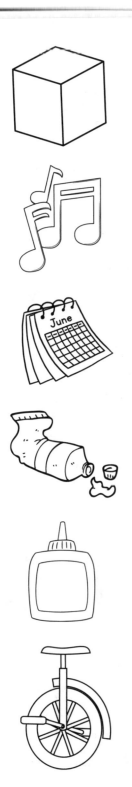

tune

tube

glue

unicycle

cube

June

Long Vowel Practice: u

Say the name of each picture out loud.
Draw a line from each picture to the matching word.

ruler

unicorn

flute

fruit

lute

mule

Read the words in the word box out loud. Read each sentence. Fill in the blank with a word from the word box.

unicorn	tune	glue	June	flute

I like the _____ .

_____ is warm.

I want to find a _____ .

I play the _____ .

The _____ is sticky.

Read each word out loud. Print the word.
Circle the picture that matches the word.

June
_____

tune
_____

mule
_____

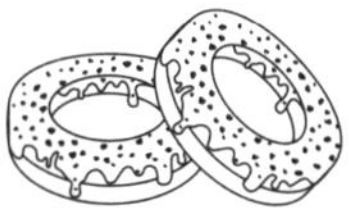

glue
_____

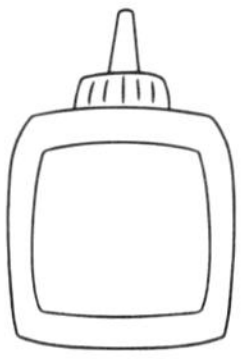

tube
_____

cube
_____

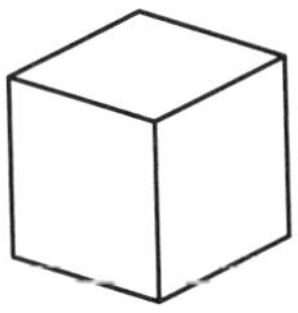

Y As Long i Sound

Sometimes the letter y makes a long i sound.

fly	sky	cry	fry

Y As Long e Sound

Sometimes the letter y makes a long e sound.

bunny	baby	lady	puppy

Y as Long Vowel Sounds: Review

Each of the words below has one of the two y sounds. Circle the correct answer for each word.

Long ē
Long ī

Long ē
Long ī

Long ē
Long ī

Long ē
Long ī

Long ē
Long ī

Long ē
Long ī

Long ē
Long ī

Long ē
Long ī

Long ē
Long ī

Long and Short Vowel Review

Say the name of each picture out loud.
Draw a line from each picture to the matching word.

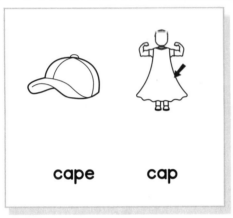

cape   cap

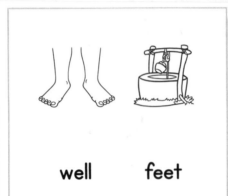

well   feet

pin   pie

June   jug

ant   ape

hog   stove

cane   can

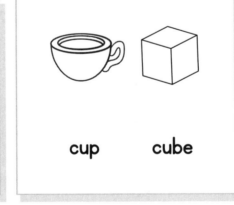

cup   cube

net   tree

Circle all the words with a long vowel.   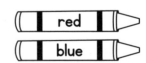 red
Circle all the words with a short vowel.   blue

Long and Short Vowel Review

Say the name of each picture out loud.
Draw a line from each picture to the matching word.

pan   cave

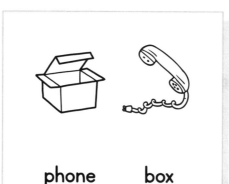

phone   box

egg   deer

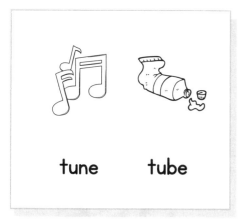

tune   tube

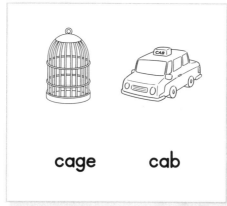

cage   cab

bed   tree

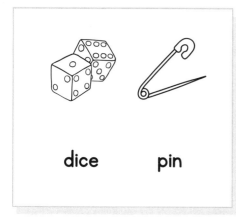

dice   pin

milk   dime

sock   rope

Circle all the words with a long vowel.   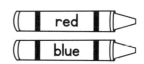 red

Circle all the words with a short vowel.   blue

Rhyming Words

Say the name of each picture out loud. Print the beginning sound to complete the word Circle the letters that make the pair of words rhyme.

_____ake

_____ake

_____ube

_____ube

_____ire

_____ire

_____ose

_____ose

_____ave

_____ave

_____one

_____one

Beginning Letter Sounds

Beginning Letters Sounds: Match up

Say the letter at the beginning of each row out loud.
Circle the pictures that begin with that letter sound.

Beginning Letters Sounds: Match up

Say the letter at the beginning of each row out loud. Circle the pictures that begin with that letter sound.

Identifying Beginning Sounds

Say the name of each picture out loud.
Colour in the beginning sound for the picture.

Identifying Beginning Sounds

Say the name of each picture out loud.
Colour in the beginning sound for the picture.

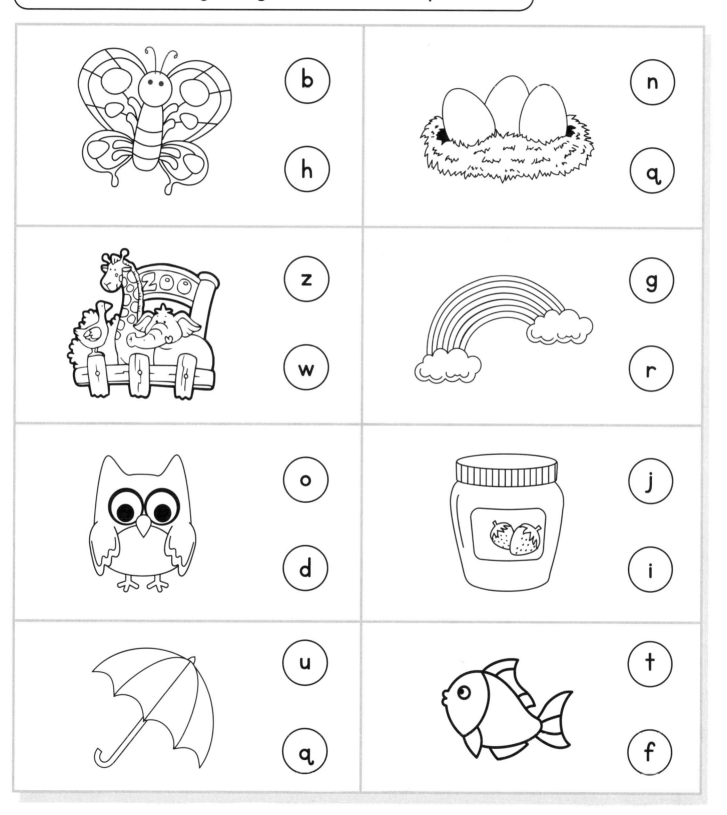

Identifying Beginning Sounds

Say the name of each picture out loud. Print the letter that shows the beginning sound for each picture name. Choose from the letters on the right.

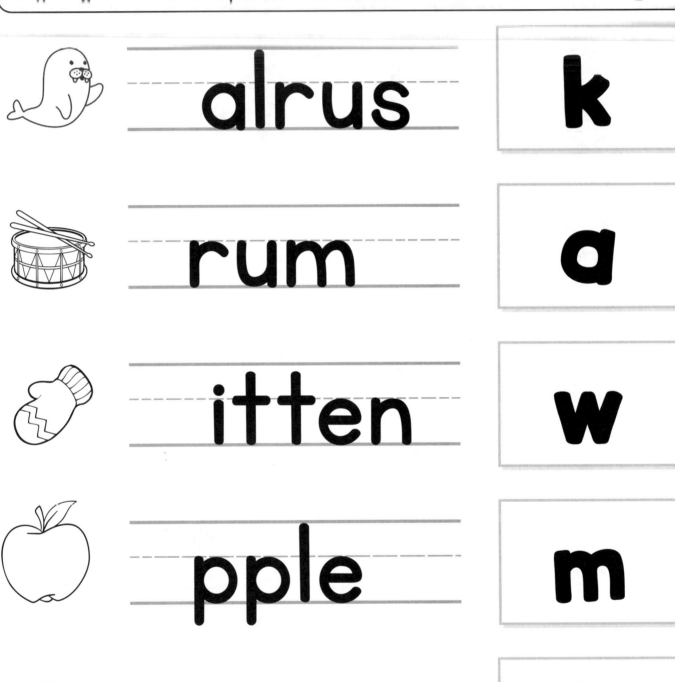

alrus   k

rum   a

itten   w

pple   m

ite   d

Beginning Sounds

Say the name of each picture out loud. Print the letter that is the beginning sound for the picture.

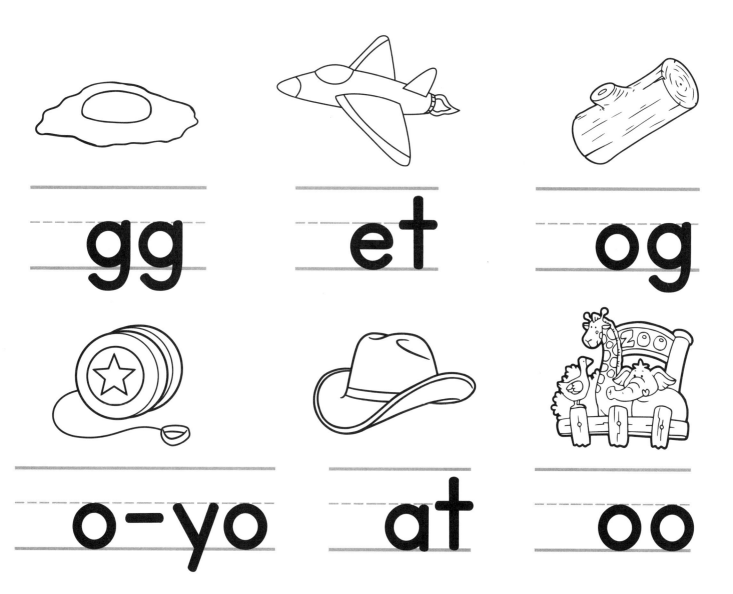

__gg

__et

__og

__o-yo

__at

__oo

Colour the egg.	black	Colour the yo-yo.	brown
Colour the jet.	yellow	Colour the hat.	orange
Colour the log.	blue	Colour the zoo.	green

Beginning Sounds

Say the name of each picture out loud. Print the letter that is the beginning sound for the picture.

uil

et

ey

wl

est

ap

Colour the quil.	red	Colour the vest.	orange
Colour the net.	purple	Colour the pan.	yellow
Colour the key.	blue	Colour the cap.	green

Beginning Letter Sounds: Match up

Say the name of each picture out loud. Draw a line to connect the pictures that have the same beginning sounds.

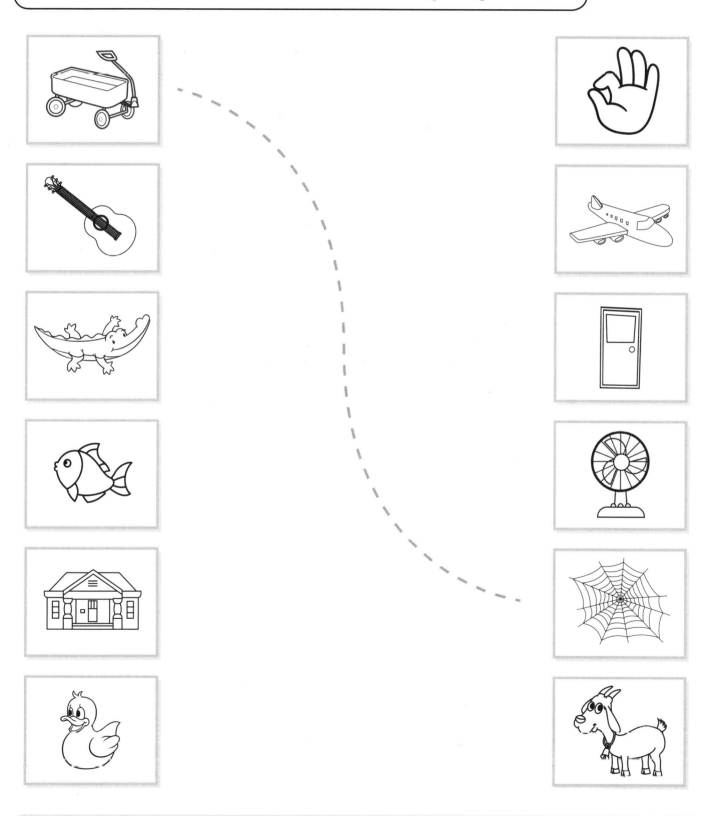

Beginning Sounds: Rhyming Fun

Change the letter that makes the beginning sound.
Print the new rhyming word on the line.

Change **cat** to  _____

Change **fun** to  _____

Change **fig** to  _____

Change **pup** to  _____

Change **pen** to  _____

Beginning Sounds: Rhyming Fun

Change the letter that makes the beginning sound.
Print the new rhyming word on the line.

Change **dog** to  _____

Change **mug** to  _____

Change **ned** to 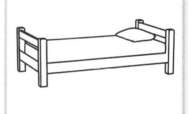 _____

Change **man** to  _____

Change **fin** to  _____

Ending Letter Sounds

Ending Letter Sounds

Say the name of the picture out loud. Colour in the ending sound for the picture.

Ending Letter Sounds

Say the name of the picture out loud. Colour in the ending sound for the picture.

Ending Letter Sounds

Circle the pictures that have the same ending sound as the word.

cat

jam

dog

mop

pen

Ending Letter Sounds

Circle the pictures that have the same ending sound as the word.

sled

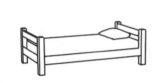 

ball

bus

ox

sip

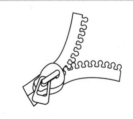  

Identifying Ending Sounds

Say the name of each picture out loud. Print the letter that shows the ending sound for each picture name. Choose from the letters on the right.

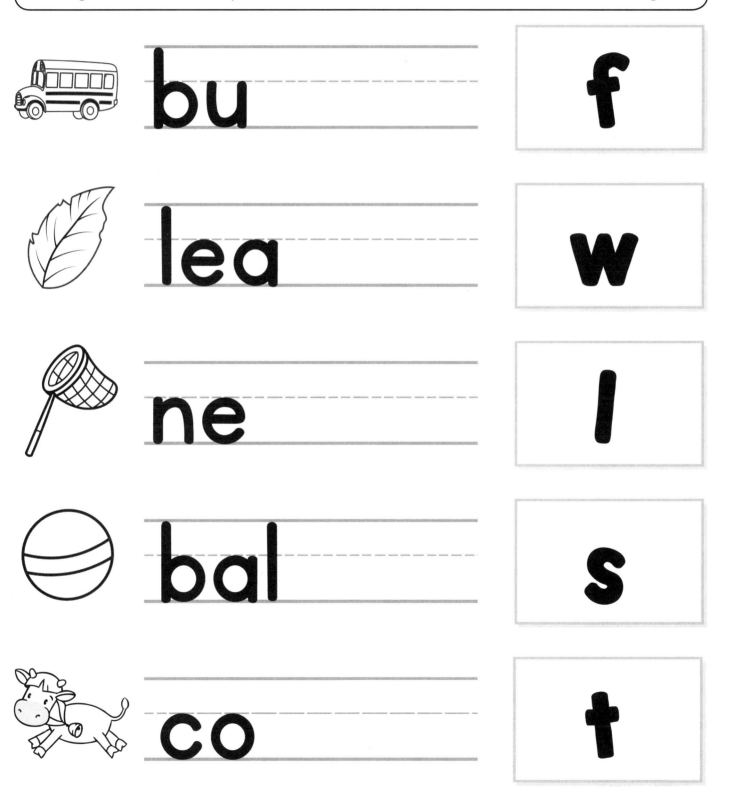

bu _____

lea _____

ne _____

bal _____

co _____

f

w

l

s

t

Identifying Ending Sounds

Say the name of the picture out loud.
Circle the ending sound for each picture.

r m p

s y x

s t w

v n r

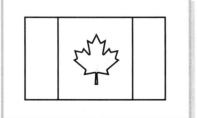

p h g

Ending Sounds

Say the name of each picture out loud. Print the letter that is the ending sound for each picture.

boo___

ba___

han___

a___

tu___

ca___

Colour the book.	black	Colour the ax.	brown
Colour the bat.	yellow	Colour the tub.	orange
Colour the hand.	blue	Colour the car.	green

Ending Sounds

Say the name of each picture out loud. Print the letter that is the ending sound for each picture.

sta

ho

pai

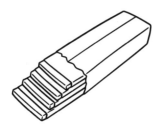

gu

fa

he

Colour the star. 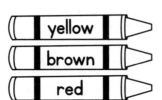 yellow	Colour the gum. black
Colour the hog. brown	Colour the fan. orange
Colour the pail. red	Colour the hen. blue

Beginning and Ending Sounds

Beginning and Ending Sounds Review

Say the name of each picture out loud. Complete the word by printing the beginning and ending letter sounds. Colour the pictures.

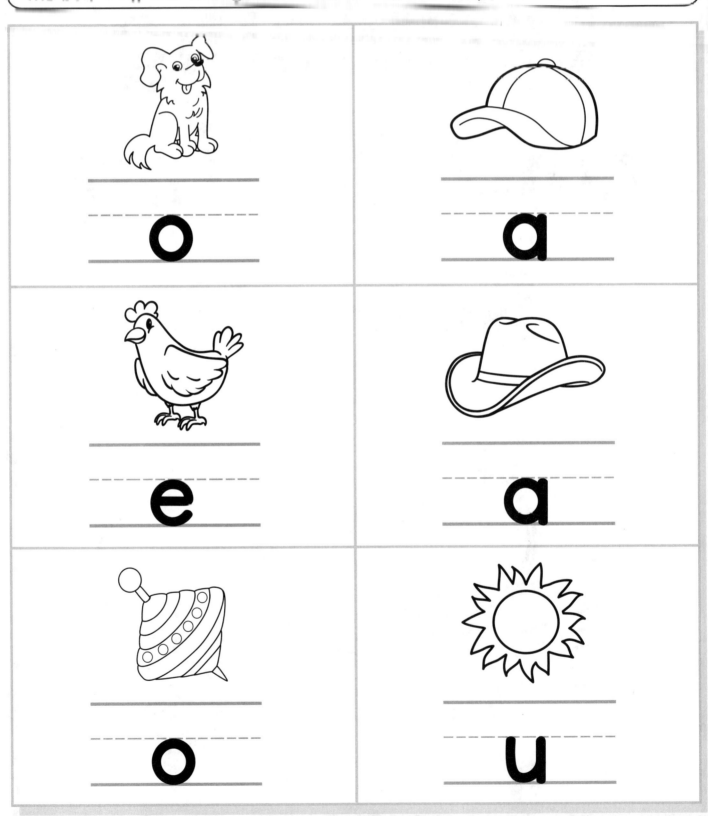

o

a

e

a

o

u

Beginning and Ending Sounds Review

Say the name of each picture out loud. Complete the word by printing the beginning and ending letter sounds. Colour the pictures.

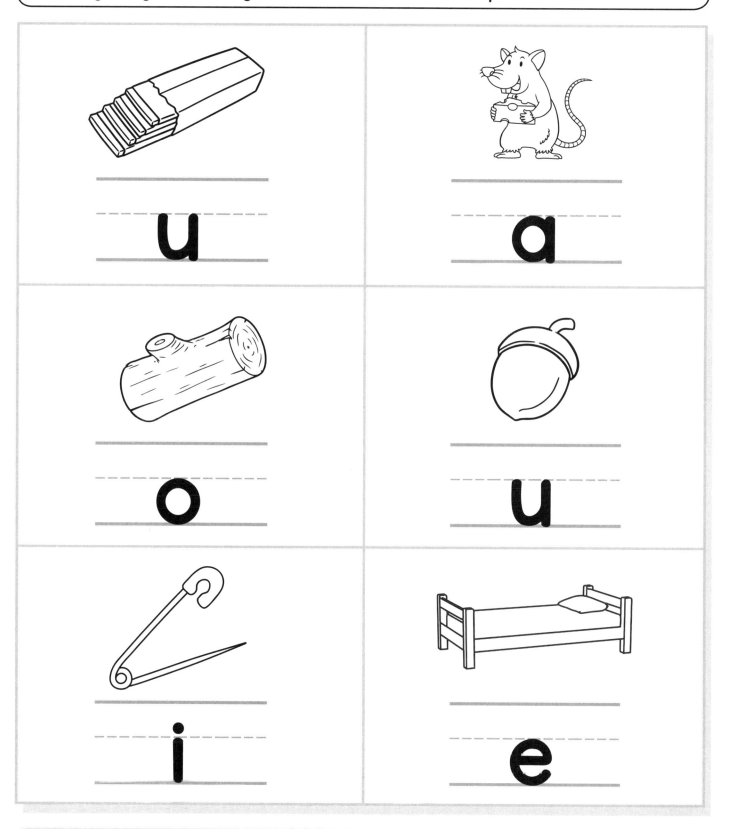

u

a

o

u

i

e

Beginning and Ending Sounds Review

Say the name of each picture out loud. Complete the word by printing the beginning and ending letter sounds. Colour the pictures.

Beginning and Ending Sounds Review

Say the name of each picture out loud. Complete the word by printing the beginning and ending letter sounds. Colour the pictures.

Consonant Blends

s blends	r blends	l blends

s blends:
- skunk
- sloth
- smile
- spill
- scarf
- snack
- star
- sweet

r blends:
- brush
- grapes
- crab
- dragon
- frame
- print

l blends:
- black
- clam
- glove
- fly
- plum

Consonant Blends With S

Say the name of each picture out loud.
Circle the correct consonant blend or beginning sounds for each picture.

sl sp	sk sc	sn sw
	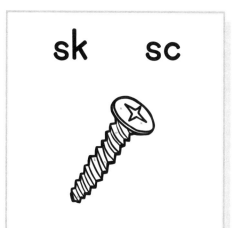	

sw sm	sl st	st sk

sw sm	sp sl	sn sk
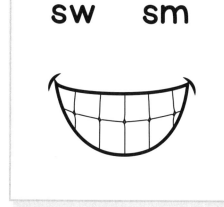		

Consonant Blends With S

sc sp	sk sw	sn st

st sl	sk sp	sm sk
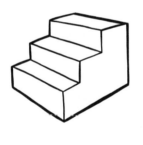		

sl sp	sk sn	sm sp

Consonant Blends With S

Say the name of each picture out loud.
Fill in the missing consonant blend or beginning sounds for each word.

sc sp	sk sp	sl sn
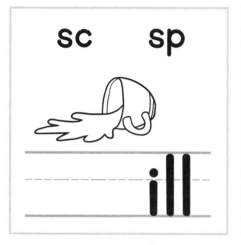		
ill	ate	ip

sl sw	sk sn	sp sl

ide	ill	ed

sm sc	sp sm	sc sm

ell	oon	ile

Consonant Blends With S

Say the name of each picture out loud.
Fill in the missing consonant blend or beginning sounds for each word.

sc sp

___ale

sk sn

___ake

sw sn

___eep

sc sp

___arf

sk sw

___im

st sn

___ar

sk st

___ep

sn sw

___ow

sc sn

___ail

Consonant Blends With S

Say the name of each picture out loud. Colour the picture with the same beginning sound as the first picture in the row.

sk				

sl				

sm				

sp				

sc				

sn				

Consonant Blends With S

Say the name of each picture out loud. Colour the picture with the same beginning sound as the first picture in the row.

st	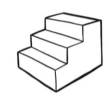			
sw				
sk				
sm				
sc				
sl				

Consonant Blends With S

Read each sentence.
Fill in the blank with a consonant blend from the word box.

sl	sm	sc	sn	st	sw

The _____ide is fun.

The _____ail is slow.

I like to _____im .

I wear a _____arf .

I wish upon a _____ar .

I can _____ell the flower.

Consonant Blends With R

Say the name of each picture out loud.
Circle the correct consonant blend or beginning sounds for each picture.

br fr	pr gr	dr cr

dr pr	dr cr	br tr

fr pr	cr fr	tr br

Consonant Blends With R

Say the name of each picture out loud.
Circle the correct consonant blend or beginning sounds for each picture.

br cr	pr tr	br fr

gr tr	cr dr	fr pr
		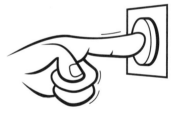

br dr	cr fr	dr tr

Consonant Blends With R

Say the name of each picture out loud.
Fill in the missing consonant blend or beginning sounds for each word.

br	gr	cr	dr	tr	pr

____ int

____ ab

____ ink

____ ead

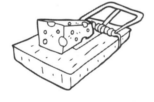

____ ap

____ as

____ ize

____ uit

____ oom

Consonant Blends With R

Say the name of each picture out loud.
Fill in the missing consonant blend or beginning sounds for each word.

br   gr   cr   dr   tr   pr

_____ y

_____ ide

_____ oom

_____ ick

_____ ash

_____ ip

_____ uck

_____ ib

_____ ane

Consonant Blends: r

Say the name of each picture out loud. Colour the picture with the same beginning sound as the first picture in the row.

br				

gr				

cr				

pr				

dr				

tr				

fr				

Consonant Blends: r

Read each sentence.
Fill in the blank with a consonant blend from the word box.

br	cr	dr	gr	pr	fr

The _____ead is fresh.

The _____ain is big.

I like my _____iend .

The _____agon is cute.

I _____ess the button.

The _____apes are tasty.

Consonant Blends With R

Say the name of each picture out loud.
Find the words. Look across for the words. Circle the words.

crab prize drip train brick grass

c	r	a	b	p	w	e
v	s	d	r	i	p	k
r	x	p	r	i	z	e
t	r	a	i	n	g	j
s	b	r	i	c	k	a
g	r	a	s	s	q	u

Consonant Blends With L

Say the name of each picture out loud.
Circle the correct consonant blend or beginning sounds for each picture.

bl pl	gl fl	bl cl
	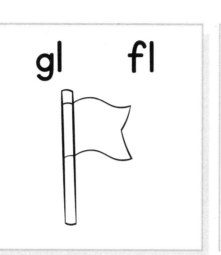	

pl cl	gl bl	fl cl

gl bl	bl pl	cl fl

Consonant Blends With L

Say the name of each picture out loud.
Circle the correct consonant blend or beginning sounds for each picture.

pl cl	fl bl	pl bl
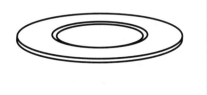		

bl fl	pl gl	cl pl

fl cl	gl cl	gl bl
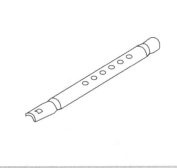		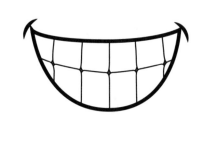

Consonant Blends: 1

Say the name of each picture out loud.
Fill in the missing consonant blend or beginning sounds for each word.

bl	cl	fl	gl	pl

_____ ack

_____ ock

_____ ove

_____ am

_____ end

_____ y

_____ ame

_____ ower

_____ over

Consonant Blends: 1

Say the name of each picture out loud.
Fill in the missing consonant blend or beginning sounds for each word.

bl	cl	fl	gl	pl

_____ um   _____ ue   _____ own

_____ ug   _____ oud   _____ anet

_____ ast   _____ itter   _____ oss

Consonant Blends: 1

Say the name of each picture out loud. Colour the picture with the same beginning sound as the first picture in the row.

bl	

cl	

fl	

gl	

pl	

Consonant Blends: 1

Read each sentence.
Fill in the blank with a consonant blend from the word box.

bl	pl	cl	gl	fl

The _____ anket is soft.

The _____ over is lucky.

I like to play the _____ ute .

The _____ ue is sticky.

The _____ anet is in space.

The _____ itter is pretty.

Consonant Blends: 1

Say the name of each picture out loud.
Find the words. Look across for the words. Circle the words.

block   clam   flag   plug   glass

b l o c k w e

v d c l a m d

r s f l a g e

p l u g h q m

d f i p w b p

t g l a s s f

Congratulations!

Great Work!

_____ **can identify:**

- **Beginning Letter Sounds**
- **Ending Letter Sounds**
- **Consonant Blends**
- **Short Vowels**
- **Long Vowels**